My Deliverance from A Life *of* Abuse

My Deliverance from A Life *of* Abuse

R L JAMES

My Deliverance from A Life of Abuse
Copyright © 2021 by R L James. All rights reserved.

No part of this publication may be reproduced, stored in a retrieval system or transmitted in any way by any means, electronic, mechanical, photocopy, recording or otherwise without the prior permission of the author except as provided by USA copyright law.

The opinions expressed by the author are not necessarily those of URLink Print and Media.

1603 Capitol Ave., Suite 310 Cheyenne, Wyoming USA 82001
1-888-980-6523 | admin@urlinkpublishing.com

URLink Print and Media is committed to excellence in the publishing industry.

Book design copyright © 2021 by URLink Print and Media. All rights reserved.

Published in the United States of America
Library of Congress Control Number: 2021901595
ISBN 978-1-64753-605-3 (Paperback)
ISBN 978-1-64753-606-0 (Digital)
24.11.20

Dear Reader,

I grew up watching Rock Hudson and Doris Day movies, which was unrealistic for a little girl who would grow up looking for her prince charming. It did not prepare women my age to deal with 'male hoes' like *Two and a Half Men*. Shows like the *Crosby*, *Family Matters*, and *Rita Rocks* are also unrealistic. Look at Whitney Houston and Bobby Brown and how drugs destroy their relationship and their careers. My ex-husband told me that I look at the world like a movie, which was true at one time until I found the love of God.

This is a little sample of what I think will make a great short story about my own life experiences. This is just one chapter of my life, and this situation happened to me within a six-month period to a year or two. I have more chapters, before and after. I have watched a lot of TV movies and TV shows. What I have to say can't be any worse. These experiences are real not made up.

I feel this may help you reader, whether you are young, old, rich, or poor, to know you can rise above a life altering experience. My dreams and hopes of living happy ever after with someone I love and who loves me but didn't turn out that way. I believed in him and believed he would do the right thing. Maybe someone out there can learn from my experiences. There is a higher power that we all have to answer to after death. Would you want to be Carl? Remember, there is more!!!!!!!!!!!!!

I have a testimony about how God changed my living situation of twenty-three years of abuse from my live-in partner. The abuse, which started in 2007, consisted of mental, physical, drugs, and alcohol that led to arrests and court hearing and everything the devil could use, through him (CARL), to come against me. I was depending on him to do the right thing by me, but the devil wouldn't let him. I was raised in the church and knew the word. I thought by the time we reach our sixties, we would be in church and serving the Lord. We both have children and grandchildren. At some point, you have to change your lifestyle to not help your children to sell drugs. I would like to be a blessing to others with my story and maybe save them from going through what I did. To be a homeless woman at the age of sixty is wrong. The Lord has something else in mind as found in Psalm 37:4 *Delight yourself also in Lord and he will give you the desire of your heart.* This is most important in this life.

MY DELIVERANCE FROM
A LIFE OF ABUSE

THE PRICE I PAID FOR LIVING IN SIN

It started one rainy Friday morning. I was standing in the doorway talking to Sharon on the phone. Across the street, were two workers landscaping the lawn in the rain. I had just said that if he came home, and his coat was not wet, I would know he just got out of a car . Then a silver car (as described in the letter) came up the street and passed the house. I ran down the steps and screamed out, "Is that her?" with the phone in my hand. I am getting ahead of myself. It started about four or five months ago, right after my mother's death and funeral. We had started having trouble around the first of the year and with my mother's passing in February, the arguing had become worse. We had started a delivering service because I was out of work. This was my only income. There were many signs of the abuse in the relationship that I chose to overlook in the years we have been together.

I remember on May 31 Memorial Day weekend, he left the house with the story he was going out with his son. He was gone for a long time and came back being very cruel to me. He said things like he wishes I wasn't here and why don't I leave. I didn't know what was going on at the time. That crushed me to the point I believe I had a nervous breakdown. I cried so hard for hours that he became scared and stopped. It was so bad the neighbor heard me crying, and one came to see if I was alright.

He used verbal abuse all the time: name-calling to lower myself esteem. Another was physical abuse at any time and for any reason at our age. Most of the arguments were about money and how much he spends on drugs weekly. We were in debt, and I had no job. He would pay one or two bills (not my bills) and use the rest on crack.

He wanted to spend the money we made from the delivery services on drugs and not pay the bills. We went to work one March morning, like always when it happened. He hit me in the head while I was driving the car in traffic. He wanted me to take him to the police after he hit me, so I did. I had to get an order from abuse on him and get a court date. He got out the next day, and things went back to normal or so it seemed. I was able to pay some of my bills, but I needed more. Then, I remember how I could get some money from my pension from a job that a work for fifteen years. After the violence, I had to move, there was no doubt about it, but I needed money to get away. Everything you hear about abuse and drugs is true, and you do see signs of it. This man had changed so fast, and he had become so cruel to me. We have been through a lot, and I always stood by him, no matter what. Most of our problems were of his creation because of drugs. We are what they call functional crack smoker. So, I applied for the money I needed and just waited for the day I could leave his crack smoking, none fucking and all the cruelty that went with it. I had no money after the book delivers ended. All I could get was food stamps. I was hoping for my unemployment to kick in, but it was going to take a while.

By now it was the first of June and Sharon, my oldest and dearest friend, had talk about the fact that Carl and I had not had sex for months. I said he was not the type of person to go without, and he wasn't asking me for it, and he liked to have sex when he is high. One warm July day, the money was transferred into my account, and it was over, so I thought. I decided to take my grandchildren to Disney world, and my sister and brother-in-law were on their way to Florida, too, with their grandchildren. It was perfect. I had the money and the time; my grandchildren had never been on a plane or been to Disney World. Carl couldn't go because of his job, and he didn't want to go.

I paid all of my bills and bought the tickets. I was scheduled to leave on Tuesday morning and stay until Sunday. On Saturday before my trip, a young lady came to the door asking for him, that was the first clue. I suspected that something was going on but couldn't prove it. So, he went out, and they talked on the porch. I was listening at the window but couldn't hear anything. They went down to the curb and continued to talk till I opened the door. He came back up and she left, so I asked him who she was and what was going on. He came up with a half-baked lie about she was from his job and came to get her keys that she left at work. I could tell he was lying, but I couldn't let him mess up my trip. The day I left, we had an argument, and he said he couldn't wait till I left. We had been getting high from the day I got the money till the day I left. I left him with money to go to his anger management meeting that the judge ordered and food till he got paid on Friday. I left my car with the kid's mother, who I could trust.

I left Pittsburgh Tuesday morning; he never called me the whole time I was gone. I was very worried but had a nice time. The time I spent away with family gave me a chance to clean up and look at the situation and how to handle the problems. I had a chance to look at my behavior and review my part in the problems we were having. I was able to understand some of the things he had been saying to me. The things I would say in a demeaning way and hateful answer that I would give him. I felt that I was going through the change of life (menopause) and that was one of the reasons I was so unhappy. This would explain some of my mood swings and the fact I felt like killing him most of the time. He had no compassion or love for me and would show it openly or would speak it often. The isolation from other people was taking its toll on me. He wouldn't go out nor have people in, so we lived in his little world. I came back determined to make this work regardless of the past; whatever was going on, it was over.

Each day I was away, I missed home more. So Sunday came, and it was time to go home. I called to let him know I was on my way back and my arrival time. I had lost some weight and my skin had become clear, being off drugs or not under stress for a week made a difference. No one had called me a stupid bitch all week or ignored me or left me sitting in house while they went out with his son (Ha!). We were about to land at the airport and as I reached across my grandson to fasten my granddaughter's safety belt, I silently spoke under my breath, "Well whatever is going on, it stops now." My granddaughter said, "Nana, what did you say?" I rushed home with excitement to see him and my pet that I had raised from the day we brought him home. I had on my red outfit, chest exposed, little shorts, socks, and running shoes. I must say I looked like a little girl, which he liked. So, we got high. He had some waiting for me, and we went and brought more for my homecoming. I wanted some sex and he liked to have sex when he is high. He was acting strange but, friendly, a little standoffish at first. I asked him what he did while I was gone, and he told me that our neighbor gave him tickets to the baseball game that Saturday and he took his son. We had a nice evening and made love. This was a test to see if he was a real dog to have sex with me after he had been with someone else. I even talked about that very fact and ask him not to do it if that was the case. If it was over, let me know now. I thought he would be a real stand up man and make the right decision.

Two days later which was a Tuesday and my birthday and I had a counseling session. I started this after the abuse in March. We had a nice meeting, and I was beginning to feel better about things. I was glad to be home, and I wanted to buy some things that I felt he had neglected to do. Maybe we would go away to our favorite places; we could go I had the money. I felt better about myself. I was no longer at his mercy if he would tell me to get out. He knew before that I had nowhere to go and no money. Things were different. I guess I felt the table had turned. I was going home to wake him up and start our day with drugs and sex or whatever he wanted. As I took the mail out of the box looking at each piece closely, I notice this handwritten letter with no return address addressed to the lady of the house. A feeling came over me from my head to my toes as I stumble in the house tearing it open, as fast as I could. I could see that the paper inside contained print instead of handwriting. As I took the letter inside out, I said out loud, "This can't be good" which made Carl start to stir from the coma he was in on the couch sleeping. He had just got off from work so while I was at my meeting, he had a chance to sleep and be ready to get started. I shouted out to him as I was reading the letter that started out with my name, and it was spelled correctly. The letter went on to say that they were our neighbors, that they liked both of us, but that my husband was having an affair with the young lady that lived down the street. The letter went on to describe that they have been watching them for over a year and heard him say that he loved her and would kiss her in front of the house. They had dates late at night, which would explain the times he would leave and come back late after the buses had stop running. The letter also said that he had tickets for the baseball game this past Saturday night and took her. By now I was reading this letter out loud for him to hear and know that now I know. The letters described the car and color where she works at and how loud she plays her music.

At that point, I had a fit and started screaming and crying like a baby for about an hour asking him question that he wouldn't answer which made me worse. So, I composed myself and went with him to get drugs. I felt I had a better chance finding out the things I needed to know and when he is high, it is easier to get an answer. I was terribly upset and everything he thought he was getting away with had been exposed, and he couldn't deny it. He's not swift enough to explain his way out. This caught him off guard; this was out of the blue, and he is not good in situations like this. Remember this was my birthday, so I went out of control for several days, abusing drugs, alcohol, food, and spending money like crazy. I was out of control, and he was scared because he didn't know what I was going to do. I thought I knew who this woman was so I started driving him by her house. I wasn't sure if it was the mother or daughter for the mother was married to a friend of my late sister and brother –in-law, and I knew him. I didn't want to go to his door with this because I knew he was ill and I wasn't sure. So, the next couple of days I just did and said what I wanted to knowing something was going to break for me. I took the letter for Sharon to read as we sat over many drinks and trying to think why he would do this and who she is, you know like girlfriends do trying to decide what my next move should be. At one point, I said that I hope that this is not part of the chapter where I am sitting in jail for killing him over his affair that was falling apart in front of his eyes. I had so much hurt and rage that I felt that it could end up like that. I knew somehow it was going to get worse, but that rainy Friday morning he called me to tell he had to work over and would be home late. He hung up before I could say anything and wouldn't answer his phone.

This is the start of the story started with me standing in the door talking on the phone about him calling two hours ago saying that he is working overtime. That was the best he could come up with. His company does not pay for overtime, and he had forgotten that I knew that. We have been together for a long time, and I knew everything about his job. So, I knew it was a lie. It was raining cats and dogs; if he was on the bus, his coat would be wet. If his coat was not wet, how would he explain that? I would know he was in a car I said to Sharon. Then, the silver car went past the house, and I could see her and the top of his hat. I was standing at the curb as he got out the car, and she continued down the street. I hung up the phone and went back inside the house to get my purse and keys. By then, he had reached the door and tried to stop me. I ran around to the back door, got into the car, and went up to where I thought she lived. Remember, the letter described her and the car. When I got there, she was hanging up the phone outside the house. I got out the car and asked her how she could do this to me; I know we don't know each other, but I thought we were friends at least girls. Then, she began to tell me about their relationship, how long it had been going on, and how he had just said he loved her. He told her that we were roommates, and she said that she thought we were related with the way he talked in the beginning. I said to her that he is at the house and asked if she wanted to go with me. She said yes, so we got into my car and went back to the house where Carl was waiting like the fool that he is. As we were driving, she told me he called her to tell her I was on my way down and to watch out that I might tell her husband about the letter and affair. He warned her. What a betrayal of our relationship. He chose her over me. She could have had a weapon or other people who would have jumped on me; he didn't know by, then we were at the house so we entered the house where he was sitting on the couch like a fool, and she began to ask him questions about his behavior or just what he was doing. Then, she said to him, "Tell her that you just said that you love me." He answered with, "Well Rose," talking to me "You know our relationship has been over for a long time." I said to him 'you love her, you love her' so loud that the neighbors heard me. I went crazy and picked up everything I could. I was going to kill him or he would kill me. I was out of control again: very violent and outraged, very verbal calling him all kind of crackheads, non- fucking motherfucker. I can't remember the things I said. I tried to hit him with anything I could find: fans, chair, incense holder, phones, brooms. I tried to spray him in the eyes with air freshener while she the other women was trying to keep me calm. She said she didn't want me to go to jail. She started begging him to leave; he was making it worst. I kept running up to him as close as she would let me, saying 'you love her.' This went on for a half hour or more until he finally left.

She began to tell me everything like how he was forcing himself on her; she also was going thought a hard time with her husband to the point she moved out. She confirmed everything that was in the letter. This had been going on for about a year but the last four months, it had got hot and heavy. The last week that I was gone, they spent all of their time together. She said that she felt sorry for the pet because he only went home to feed him and then leave. She told me about the tickets to the baseball game, but she refused to go he wanted her to go. She told me that the young girl that came to my house that Saturday night was her daughter; she sent her there to get her key that he had took from her. I told her a lot of things about him and our relationship, but the main thing I told her was that I was not leaving, and he couldn't make me. We talked for hours and smoked cigarettes. When I felt I had all the information I needed to nail his ass to the wall, we exchanged numbers. We agreed that she would call me when he called to make a date. Little did I know the worst was still to come.

So, the next morning she called me to tell me that Friday night after she left work Carl and his son came up to her apartment. She and Carl stood in the parking lot and talked. He told her that he loved her and could not take it if she was with someone else. He would kill her and then Carl started to cry. They made plans to meet on Saturday for lunch; he would call her and tell her where to meet him. She was calling me so I could be there when they met. Remember, she is trying to be my friend and help me out (what a lie). Carl called me Saturday morning to pick him up at 7:00am like any other day and when we returned home, he went right to sleep on the couch while I went to my appointment to get my nails done. On my way home, she called me again about their lunch plans. When I went in the house he was still sleeping, so I slammed the door very hard so he would wake up. I asked him what we were doing today to see what he would say. He lied like he had been doing from the beginning of this whole affair. He said we could do or go anywhere I wanted. So, I said, "Don't you have a lunch date with Princess Grace?" and I told him everything she said that happened the night before. He lied and said none of it was true. That he didn't go to her apartment Friday night with his son, and he didn't even know where she lived, which was a lie. He also said he didn't want to have anything else to do with her ever again. So, I have two people telling me different versions of the truth. Which one should I believe? This was a very cruel thing for someone to do to another person. I have never treated any one in my life like this and would never do this to someone that I had been with for a long period of time. I could not believe that he would treat me so badly. But after beating me up and being on drugs, I should have expected this type of behavior. So, for the next two days, she rode up and down the street with her music playing loud so we would know it was her. Remember, she lived down the street and had a husband that I knew very well, but that didn't stop her from harassing me every chance she got pretending to be my friend and trying to help me with my self-esteem issue. I didn't have that issue until now. He had told her that she was so fine, and he wanted to show her off to all his friends but couldn't do that with me because I was so ugly and old. She was about four or five years younger than me. Before this happened, I didn't have any self-esteem issues about my looks. I was always able to get whoever I wanted without any trouble, including him. Most of the men I went out with were better looking than him, and some were younger and they were crazy about me. I didn't realize at that time that my relationship with him would ever be the same again, and that there was no future for us because of what he had done, by putting me in this situation. That Sunday we started our day by getting dressed to go out with our dog, shop, and buy drugs for the day as we did every day. When we were coming back to the house, her car came up behind us like she was waiting for us to return. She stopped her car in the middle of the street as I was parking, got out, and told me to tell Carl

My Deliverance from A Life of Abuse

to give her back her house keys, because he had took them when he was at her house the week I was out of town. I didn't mention that she was separated from her husband but still stayed at their house sometimes, and she had her own apartment to have sex in. She told me they were trying to work things out in their relationship. They were having hard times and that is how Carl was able to sweet talk her. I know he is good at catching you at your lowest point. That how I met him, when I was trying to break-up with my other friend at the time. Looking back on it, I should have stay where and who I was with. She claimed to be very upset about her marriage and needed someone to talk to, and he seemed to be a nice guy, but they are the same type of people. They use people for their own needs and toss them away like bags of trash when they're done with you, and they don't care who they hurt in the process. Her husband was very sick and if he knew what was going on, it would have hurt him very badly if not killed him. He also knew Carl as well. They would talk when they see each other. How could two people be so ruthless? I had to keep this to myself I could not be the one to tell her husband what was going on. Back to the situation that was going on in the middle of the street… Carl went into the house and brought the keys out and gave them to her in front of me and the whole neighborhood. I tried to talk to him about it when we went in the house, but he just sit there smoking his crack and not saying a word. I thought that would be the end of this problem, I was wrong. She continued to ride up and down the street and would call Carl on his phone at work. I guess she stopped calling me because I didn't leave. I told her I wasn't going to leave, and Carl or her couldn't make me leave. Looking back on it I should have left. I was so confused and hurt. My mother had just died, I didn't have a job, and I wasn't going to be outdone by him or her. It was not worth it because I lost a lot of me, and I will never be the same person I was before. Believe me, it gets worse. How I could have loved someone that could torture me and hurt me in so many ways. I thought he was a special person, and I wanted to spend the rest of my life with him. I had been with him in bad times as well as good times. Whatever life would send our way, we would be together like we were in the beginning. I was always there for him even before he started to abuse me in one way or another. Summer was over; it was September and I was trying to put all this behind me and thought he was trying to. I wanted to believe that until one day, he was out of the car buying crack and his phone rang. I didn't answer it, but I listened to the message. It was her saying she had just left the doctor office, that she was pregnant, and that she needed him to call her back right away. When he got back into the car, I was in the middle of another breakdown and went off on him about this pregnant woman. His response was that she would be pregnant by herself because he didn't believe her and didn't care. The thing that got to me was the fact he was out here having unprotected sex with someone he didn't know at his age and would come back and have sex with me. This was really a statement of how he felt about me, for real. I did step out on him one time, at the beginning of our relationship when I wasn't sure I would stay with him, but I was very responsible and and after it happen I decided to stay with him, I never did it again; I could have, but I didn't. I am not that distrustful or two-faced as some people are. I was taught to do the right thing always. There were men I was involved with that if I had treated them like I treated him I would have had a better life than the life I have now with him. I made a huge mistake; I didn't know how huge it would turn out to be until now, and it is still going on. She would ride up and down the street during the winter months playing the music loud so we would know it was her, but I didn't hear anything else about the pregnancies, so I thought she was lying like he said. I wanted to believe that so badly. I can't explain why I didn't leave Carl after all of that had happened. I didn't, so I guess I got what I was looking for- unhappiness. The people that found out about what he has been doing or the ones that I told lost all respect for him. They use to look up to him and trusted him; they would come to him for advice. They thought he was one of the good guys, and I thought that too; I guess that was my problem, too. People in my family living and dead would have been very disappointed in him and his treatment of me. He had made several promises to some of my family members that are no longer here that he would take care of me. I know they are looking down on him in disbelief. They all welcome him into my family and tried to make him feel part of it. . I would take him to dinners and cookouts, Christmas, all the holidays. There were a couple of times my car was in the shop and Carl needed a ride home from work, my friends Sharon would go and pick him up and take him to the store. They would do whatever we needed. I am so sorry I subjected any one of them to him; everyone treated him nice, even some of my co-workers. I was so proud to be with someone like him. I guess I thought more highly of him then I should have, which is the wrong way to think, because no one is better than anyone else.

The money I received had just about run out, but I was holding on to a couple bucks for Christmas. I wasn't worried about money because it was getting closer to spring, and we would start up our delivery service once again. Our relationship had taken a big hit with the news of a baby even though he said it was not true. He told me he discussed it with one of his friends who said he would put a gun in her mouth to make her have a miscarriage, and Carl laughed. He thought it was funny. I guess I really started to look at him differently. She was someone that Carl said he loved, and he was willing to hurt me for this woman. When she needed him where was he laughing at her problem? I was beginning to see there was no future for me and him anymore. I just didn't want to let go just yet. March came and we started our delivery business. Again, he promised it wouldn't be like last year where he had to go to jail for hitting me, and I believed him. When you reach a certain age changing is hard to do. So, I went along with him, and we made it to the last month of the delivery business. The work was seasonal, and we had two days before it was over. On that last Sunday, he started an argument with me and asked me to take him back home, so I did. He was calling me all kind of names out in public like bitch and many other things. I went back to work after dropping him off and when I returned, it started again. Before I knew it, he had punched me in my mouth and blackened my eye and knock out my front tooth. I ran upstairs where I could get away and call the police. He knew I was calling, so he left the house. I gave a report to the police, and they went looking for him. He still had a PFA on him for three years. I didn't hear from him until later on that evening when he called to find out if they were looking for him. He wanted to come and get his work bag and some clothes so he could go to work on Monday. I told him they were looking for him and he could come and get his items. I would leave them on the porch. As far as I was concerned, this was it. He had done so much by this time to me to let it go again. So, Carl turned himself in and went to jail for the night. His son paid his bond and Carl called me when he was released. He asked if he could come home and help with the last of the delivery and to tell me he was sorry and asked if I would not show up for the hearing. He did not want to go to jail because this was his second time in two years, and he would have to get a lawyer to get him out of this one. I let him come back to help because it was in my name, and I had to complete this assignment if I wanted to work next year. We delivered the item and went to buy drugs then came back to the house to smoke.

Our day to day living had become quite different and unpleasant. I grew tired of trying to please him, and it was started to show. So, we took on another job that summer, that we could work on together; it was a seasonal job, which was very stressful and brought out all the bad feeling along with the memory of his relationship with that woman. It came out again, and the physical abuse started again. I had to call the police again, so he had to leave the house. Guess whose house he went to stay at. He was at her house and she called and asked me if I would tell him to leave because she did not want him there. So, she put him on the phone. I told him to come home, and I would not call the police. When he came home, he tried to explain that he had nowhere else to go and all he wanted to do was to sleep so he could go to work.

The next day she started calling me again. She went from stalking me to acting like we were friends again. What type of women does that? She told me that Carl started telling her that when he met me, I was desperate for a man which was a lie because I had someone else at the time, but that is another story. So, I told Carl everything she told me and made up a couple new things so he would not want her. I thought it worked for a long time until the next year in the spring when they started up again. We started having a hard time again and we were working the job that brought out the stress in our relationship. He had a pattern when he was having an affair, which meant he would treat me like crap, like I was a worthless human.

I could always tell. Carl was the type of person that after he has used you for what he wanted, then he throws you away. I watched him do it with other people. I never thought he would do it to me. When it first came out about this affair, it took him less than a minute to turn on her. He had stood in the living room and told me that in was in love with her and when he found out that she was spilling everything about the affair, then he changed. So, we started fighting again. I was tired of the ups and downs with him and her. So, when he went to work, and I knew she was at work; they both worked at night. That was how they could arrange to meet each other while they were supposed to be at work. I found out later that he would have me drive him to work and would meet her around the corner. He hardly spent any time with me; he would never call off or take vacation day to be with me but, took time to be with her. She told me he would tell her personal things about me when they were together. The betrayal was too much to take, and it was making me sick inside to know that he was the person I was in love with and had love for many years.

He had brought this woman, who is not my friend, back into my life again. When he came back, I did not say a word and let him go sleep so he could go to work. That night I had a plan. I was going to move and take everything from the house; it was all mine anyway. The next day, she called again to talk to me because she felt so bad about this happening again. I asked her why she took him in. She said because they were friends and, so by this time, I said enough is enough. He keeps abusing me for nothing, treating me like dirt and after everything he said about her, he went and stayed at her house. Remember, he said he didn't know where she lived and had never been in her house. I know the things he does with his mouth and other parts of his body, and he can only have sex when he is high. I guess he thought she would have sex with him but she refused. They had a fight so to fix him, she called me to tell me what he was up to. What type of friendship did they have when every step of the way, she continued to make things worse for him? First, it was the letter. Then, coming down to the house with me to confront him, and she was just getting started or so she thought. She told me about the baby and said that Carl brought her the money to get rid of it. This could be true I don't because he could have gotten the money from family or friends. I told her what he said about sticking the gun in her mouth to make her lose the baby and how she would be pregnant by herself. She wanted to know why I still stayed there with him after everything he has done. It was really was none of her business (the bitch). I have my own friends, and they are not people who stab you in the back like she was doing every time he gave her any information about me. Before I knew about this affair, she would ride up and down the street smiling in my face and greeting me with hello and asking how my day was going. You have to watch out for people like that. I knew their time was coming to an end. Carl didn't realize this until it was too late. I will never forget what he has done to me. I don't know what is worse: the abuse or the deceitfulness or lies or that woman trying to pretend she cared about me that made me sick, sick. I wanted to go to heaven, or I would have killed them a long time ago, but I have another plan for her and him. Remember, her husband is a friend of my family, and I did not want to be the one to hurt him because he was ill. He is a very nice man and when I was younger, I had a crush on him, but I never did anything about it because he was married to his first wife who I liked. When you have been raised properly you don't go around wrecking people's life and hurting them for your own pleasure. There is a higher power that we all have to answer to, and I didn't want that to come up for me. You should treat people the way you want them to treat you. There is so much killing in this world today because people have no morals or compassion or kindness. So, I listened to everything she had to say and I learned quite a lot about this woman. Carl wanted to know why I would listen and I told him why: to hear all the lying that was going on between the two of them. How he could want someone likes her, I will never know why. I guess because she was nice looking. Beauty is only skin deep, and the rest of her was ugly. She would have done to Carl worse than what she did to her own husband. One day, Carl told me he believed she had fucked every man on her job. She was pretending to be a faithful wife every day and while having affair with the man right down the street. She was smiling in her husband's face like Carl was smiling in my face. Who knows what other man she had or was using like this? I still carry around the letter that was mailed to my house on my birthday. We know she wrote it or had someone else do her dirt work. Carl did tell me that he told her to leave me alone and I believe that is why she did it. I waited until things quieted down before I started with my plan. Yes, I had a plan. I hated to do things this way but, they (Carl and Princes Grace) gave me no choice. I started calling her that name because of the way she acted. I didn't go to the hearing, so the charges were dropped. I didn't have any money or a job, and I wanted to leave so bad. I could have stayed with family and friends, but I didn't want to, It wouldn't have been right. Carl still had the PFA on him for one more year. All I had to do was call the police and say he was abusing me again, and they would come because he wasn't allowed in the house. She was still calling me every day, and I was tired of it. I had saved some of her messages and went to see her husband with the letter that was mailed to me that kept saying over and over again that they thought I needed to know. Well, I thought he needed to know what his wife and Carl had been doing with each other and me behind his back. After discarding things in the basement for the trash man, I went down the street for a visit with her husband and my friend. He wasn't home so I waited. I had decided to wait for him for half an hour. If he didn't come back by then, I would leave and try to contact another time. While I was sitting there going over the plans for my escape from the misery that I had sunk into, I thought about the last two years of my life and how I know some of it was my fault for staying in this dead-end relationship. But in my defense, I had never met a group of ruthless people like this in my life. I have never been involved with any man that would treat me this way and the name calling. No one have ever said such rotten and nasty things to me in private or public. They would never say things that Carl has said to me and is still saying. There was one time in the beginning of this abusive relationship, he said to me, in the heat of an argument we were having, that if he had to choose between me and his family, I would lose. I don't want to get ahead of myself. There is lot more to tell and a lot more happened. My plans were: first, I would tell my friend (her husband) then, I would go to the counseling service the city offered and see if I could find a place to stay. I had already packed and made arrangement with a moving company to come and leave a storage container for me to put all my things in. They would take the container back to their company for a month or two. Just then my friend pulled up with a puzzled on his face. He was wondering why I was sitting in front of his house. All the years I live down the street, I never visited him and her. I had often thought about it when I would see them two together. It would have been nice to be friends with her and for Carl to be friends with him. They looked like a nice couple and because I had a history with him from the past, it would have been perfect. He had been a friend of my family from the time I was a little girl and was around me when I in my teens. I am so glad I did not try to make things happen. I got out the car and asked him how he felt and told him that he was surprised to see me there. I said I was sorry that I haven't been down to see him before now. I told him I had a story to tell him, but I wanted to know if he had been the one who sent me a letter. He said no. I could tell he didn't have a clue about what I was talking about. The look on his face as we sat down on the porch will never leave me, and I took out the letter and let him read it. After he was finished, I told him I hated to be the one to tell him what his wife had been up to. I told him all the nasty things she and Carl have been doing behind his back. He started asking me about my life with Carl: things that we like to do, what we did for fun, and how we lived. I told him about the things we did: computers, traveling, watching the history channel, researching events, and family history on the internet. We were a couple so we did things that couples did. His response was he didn't understand why Carl would want his wife because she was not into any of that stuff and would find it boring. I said it must have been about sex only. I let him listen to the messages on my phone of her describing parts of her relationship with Carl, which was not pleasant, but he listened to all of it any way. That's why you should watch what type of messages you leave with people on a cell phone. He started telling me about his relationship with Carl that I didn't know about. He told me how they talk about going into business together and maybe working on the delivery service because both of them were businessmen, and my friend had owned his own business at one time. He told me he thought Carl was a stand-up guy, and he wanted to work with him never dreaming he was stabbing him in the back with his wife. He said he did not know this was going on, and they would meet outside when Carl would be taking our dog out for a walk. He said he had told Carl about how long he has known my family and his relationship with my family and if we needed anything to just ask. He picked up his cell and called another old friend of the family to come over right away; it was very important. This was someone I knew also a close friend of the family too, and the two of them had been friend ever since they were little boys together. When these two men were younger, they were a force on the street and a danger to whoever got in their way. They were no jokes and to make a fool of one, you were in trouble with the other one and everyone else they could and would call. Carl thought he was a force as well but not in this area because no one knew him the way that they were known. There is a street code, and Carl had broken every one of them. You don't mess around with someone's wife and smile up in that person's face. He said he told Carl that I was like his little sister, and he would do anything to see that I wasn't hurt now that I lived on his street, he can watch over me; he was glad that I had someone like Carl. He even told me there were times he would come out the house and his wife and Carl would be talking like neighbors do about the weather or pets, you know things that neighbors talk about. Then, a car pulled up, and his friend stepped out the car. This was very hard for me, and I was smoking like crazy, not crack. I had stopped smoking for over a month; I knew I needed to get a job, so I had to quit for all my plans to fall into place. After we explained everything that was going on, they, of course, wanted to find Carl and go to work on him. I convinced them to let me take care of Carl my way and told them of my plan. So, we agree not to say anything till after I move and was no longer in the neighborhood and after that, they could do whatever they want to him. I just asked one favor: don't hurt the dog. They agreed, and I left and went back home to continue with my plan. I didn't have to worry about Carl. He was at work, and he didn't have to worry about his wife; she was at work. I really didn't think about this before: they both work at night, how convenient. The next morning, I had to run downtown and I just happened to see a friend from years ago who works with Carl at night, and she told me some interesting things about him. She confirmed the fact that one evening after I had dropped him off at work, he didn't work. He had taken a vacation day. That woman had also told me the same story. He had taken a vacation day and after I had dropped him off, she picked him up, and they went to her apartment and spent the night together. The next day, he came home like he went to work like always, the deceit never stopped. Her husband thought she went to work, too. In the morning, she came home and checked on him like she always did after work; he had a medical condition and was older than all of us. I can remember him saying she was walking around like the loving wife. My friend promised me he would wait until I moved, but I guess he couldn't and when she came home the next morning, he let her have it. She never expected me to tell him and that was her plan: to stay close with me and to pretend she was a friend so that I would not tell. She didn't know me, and I let her think her plan was working until I couldn't take her phone calls anymore. It was like I was being harassed by both of them. Knowing what he had did and listening to what he was doing with her made me sick to my stomach, and I had to make it stop before I had another nervous breakdown. My plans were falling into place except the next morning as I was on my way to the meeting with the counsel, Princess Grace called me on the phone and said that they were on their way down the house to talk with me and Carl. She left that message on my phone, I kept driving to my appointment and what happened would have to happen. Carl was at the house and didn't know I had told her husband, and they were on their way down to talk. While I was waiting to see the counsel, I called the police just in case. I didn't want anyone to get hurt and her husband was known to carry a gun. I went to my appointment and made arrangements to enter into the shelter that Sunday night; it was Thursday. As I was going back home, my cell phone rang. It was Carl. He had survived the situation from that morning with the happy couple coming down to talk about their affair and he ask me if the police was looking for him to lock up. He told me they talked outside, and Carl told my friend how sorry he was (what a pile of shit). He was sorry he got caught. After they left, the police came. He ran out the back door and jumped over the fence to get away. I listened and found out what I needed to know: he was out of the house and wouldn't come back. He was too scared to return. I did tell him he could come back on Saturday after I hung up the phone. Next was the third part of my plan, to move all my things in the container (POD) in one day and be gone by Saturday. So, I started moving things in and calling around for help. Some of my family came to help the next day and by that Friday evening, all my stuff was packed away and what I couldn't get in the container or in the car, I destroyed. I took the curtains down from the windows. I have never been in a situation like this before and it was over, and all I had to do is leave and start my new life. I received a call from my friend, and he started to describe everything that went on that morning between his wife and Carl when they came down to the house. It was not pretty. He told me that she said, after they left the house that Carl couldn't get it up. All he could do was use his nasty mouth on her and that Carl was on crack. She also said she didn't love Carl, and he forced himself on her. She also said Carl told her lies about me. My friend said that his wife was a liar too and that no one should believe anything that she said. He also said that she used to run around before they got married and with other men, he had caught her. I asked him why did he married her. He said he fell in love and could not help it. His friend told me when we were at his house and he had went in the house to take his medicine that nobody in his family liked her, and he wasn't surprised what was going on when I down his house talking to them. He had heard a lot of things about her and knew a lot more and none of which were good. I felt that he might have had an affair with her, or she had approached him or someone else he knew. One of the messages I let him listen to was about the baby she said she was going to have and how much Carl paid to make it go away. When he asked his wife about it, she denied everything. She didn't know he had heard her on phone talking to me about the problem and when he told her he knew everything, she started crying and asking for forgiveness. He told her she was messing with my life and asked how she could do this to someone's family. He said he asked her what type of person is she. He didn't think they would stay together after this, and it would be too hard to fix. They were already having troubles because he couldn't trust her. I am so sorry I had to do this, but I felt better that it was out, and everyone involved knew what was going on not just me. I had been living in silence for a long time. Carl and his women were getting away with it and torturing me at the same time, making a fool out of me and my friend. He is a nice guy and didn't deserve this treatment from her or Carl, and it had to stop before someone got killed. There was a chance that he would have found out on his own or a neighbor would tell him. Someone wrote that letter that said all the neighbors knew about it. I think that she wrote it or had someone else do it. We talked for a while, and he wanted to know my plans after I leave. So, I told him about staying in the shelter until I could get a job and then an apartment. I told him I would be fine. He asked me if I loved Carl; I hated to say yes. I told him I would get over Carl and not to do anything to get in trouble because the two liars aren't worth going to jail for life. I made him promise me, and I told him I would keep in touch. I had started drinking and was feeling no pain. After everyone left, I went into each room looking around and crying. It was just me and the dog I had grown to love with all my heart. I hate what Carl had done with a passion; he was destroying my life along with all my hopes and dreams for a piece of ass that he couldn't even get hard enough to have sex with. Just how sad is that, and she was telling everyone she knew that he couldn't get it up. The things he has done to me could never be repaired, and I can't go back in time when he was a decent guy, a standup guy, someone that I loved very much and would love even if he couldn't have sex. The only thing I can say is the drugs turned him, or he was always like this but I just couldn't see it. There wasn't anything in the house to sit on, so the dog and I sat on the floor while and I continued to drink. Then, I called Carl to let him know he could come back Saturday morning. The dog would be in the house by itself because I couldn't take him with me to the shelter. Carl asked me was I trying to get him killed and why did I tell her husband. My answer was (I thought he needed to know) liked it said in the letter to me. Then he asks me did I send the police to the house. My answer was yes so you didn't get killed. I really wanted him out the house so I could pack. We said a couple more things, and then he hung up on me. I was so drunk by then that I lay on the floor with the dog and went to sleep; this is what Carl had reduced me to. I feel that with all my heart that you are accountable for the thing you do on this earth and things you do to people. You cannot just destroy a person's life and get away with it. Some way and somehow you have to answer for what you have done to a person or people. When I awoke the next morning, I kissed the dog and made sure everything was locked up and left. I called to make sure he would go back to the house to take care of the dog. He wouldn't answer the phone so I went down to his job. They were just getting out of work, so I drove up to him and asked him if he was going home to take care of the dog. He said yes while trying to look in the car to see what I had in there. I have lost so much by being with him, for example: time, family and friends. I never asked him to give up anything on account of me. That is not the way I was raised and not the way my family was toward him. I would never ask anyone to do anything like that. There is so much more; I can see now that it is really over. So much more I could have done with my life, so much life I could have lived. I let myself get caught up in this nightmare he called a life. I just never knew how one could be so cruel to another person. I could go into more detail but for now we will let it go. That is another chapter I can write about later. He pretended to be a different type of person in the beginning. It wasn't just me that thought that. A lot of other people told me that also- men and women. Looking back at all of the things and promises that he said to me, all the places we would go: they were all lies because the drugs were more important to him than anything else. I drove away and went to stay with a friend, who let me stay until it was time for me to check in at the shelter. When he returned to the house and seen that everything was gone, he started calling me on the phone. He continued to call and call all day long; at one point, I turned my phone off so I could get some sleep. When I woke up and turned my phone back on, he had been calling me so many times that I finally answered. He started asking me why did I take this and why did I take that. I told him because I paid for it. The things he paid for I left there which was not much because all his money went to drugs. Remember, he buys crack with his money not food, not even clothes, and no soap or paper towel, tooth pastes, cleaning materials. He won't even wash his clothes. These are things we would fight about all the time. I had to buy all these things and more because I can't live like a crack head, but it was fine with him. I know there would be some sad stories about the way we live. If I could not to get a job or had ways of making some money. He is a crack head for real because eating is not in his plan at all and going to the store to shop is something he never wanted to do. He just wants to get his drugs and go home to smoke and have sex when he could. He never thought about his health or mine or what this was doing to our bodies. I can say for sure he turned me out and I let him. I was no angel but I had priorities, and drugs was low on my list not first. One Christmas, I can remember that I had just started working and would not receive a pay in time for the holidays and I ask him to loan me some money until I got paid so we could have a nice holiday and buy presents. We both had families to buy for, and he didn't care about things like that. Let's just say the drug dealer had a good Christmas thanks to Carl, and I saw the result of the drug money Carl spent with him, the drug dealer, because he was able to buy his kids all kinds of toys and bikes and a home entertainment center. Carl let me have some money but not much. I had to pay it back and when I did get paid, he took it and bought more crack and then ate what even food I had cooked for the holiday. If it hasn't been for me, he wouldn't have things and even a place to live. I help him every step of the way, and this is how he treats me after all of the years we have been together. I know you don't do things for the reward and that wasn't why I did those things. I like to help people, and I have always been that way. So here I am now: nowhere to live and no job, and I had to go to the shelter the next day. Do you have any idea how low I felt but for the grace of God I would have killed myself or Carl? The next day around eight o'clock, I check myself in the shelter but before that I went to church with another family member. I felt the need for prayer; I was scared this was something I had never gone through before. I didn't know what to expect, and I missed my dog. I knew Carl wouldn't take care of him like I did. He claimed he loved him, but the truth is there is only one thing he loved on this earth and it wasn't me or the dog. It was and still is drugs. Carl continued to call me on the phone and the people at the shelter told me not to answer it and to turn the phone off. They have seen this type of behavior before, and they told me I could call the police and tell them he was harassing me. They also told me to save all of his messages as proof of him calling, so I did. They assigned me a room with another person and I sat on the bed and cried for a long time, thinking about the events from the last year up until this point and wandering how he could do this to me. We have been together for a long time and went through a lot of stuff, some good and some bad. I always had his back; I went through hell and high water to help him every time. There was no one else standing in line to help him, and I didn't do it for him to help me. I did because I loved him and thought he loved me. I never thought he would stab me in the back or mistreat me to the point I would have to go to a shelter. What type of man is this and why did I let him into my life to hurt me this way? I know that I am not the only woman that has been mistreated, beaten and even killed. So, when you see a sign of a no-good man, run. Do not walk away from him, run. This is your life and you can't get the time back that you wasted, and it is not worth it. This is helping me by telling my story to others who can learn from this and not make the same mistake. This is for the old and young, this is for women, young girls, as well as men. When you hear reports about the signs of drug abuse and what it can lead to, you should listen and take steps so nothing like this can happens to you or a loved one. It does destroy a person's brain cells making one unable to distinguish what is right and what is wrong. After a while, all they care about is the next high, where they will get the money, and how it makes them feel. I am not blaming everything on drugs; he was on drugs before we became involved. I started smoking crack because of him, but I didn't need it like he did. I like buying clothes and eating, and I can make love without being high. I know some people are weak and can't help themselves but using something that will make you treat a person like shit, I would have to let it go. Carl can go to work and do his job, and he does it well. He could go and talk with his bosses, and they would never know that he was on drugs. He is and will always be a crack head, and he is proud of it. A very nice lady told me long time ago that when I prayed for a man you have to ask God for a certain type of man not just a man, and I forgot that when I asked God to send me someone. I didn't say what type, and this is what I ended up with. So, the next day I went to all the meetings, and I had already applied for a job before I went to the shelter. They call me that afternoon to go downtown and take a drug test. My prayers were starting to be answered. I knew I would pass the drug test because I had stop long time ago, and this meant I had a job. I went to the testing center and returned to the shelter to wait for a call on my starting date. Later that afternoon, they called and told me I could start that next Monday, and it would be for six months to a year. I was so happy and things were looking up so when the phone rang again and it was Carl, I answer it and started telling him my good news. That was my first mistake and there are many more to come. This story is not over yet; he had some more surprises for me. I would have been better off if I had changed my cell number. I didn't so that left me open to his empty promises and more lies. I needed to know how the dog was doing. I miss him (the dog) so much and I know he miss me. So, Carl said he was glad for me about the job and started telling me how the dog was missing me. This made me cry, and I started looking around at the place I had landing in which made it worse. I can remember telling Carl I would never forgive him for what has happened to me. Carl had made a promise to my aunt on her death bed that he would take care of me and look how he has kept his promise. I always thought that your word is your bond, and a man and woman stand by their word; I am a woman of my word. Carl started to talk to me about how sorry he was and how he wishes that I would come back. I couldn't believe the things he was saying after everything he had put me through. Carl said he would never do it again, and he would spend the rest of his life making it up to me, and things would change if I come back. He said he didn't know why he did it, and that he had a weak moment, and that is how Princess Grace became part of our life. Looking back on it, they were blaming each other because they are the same: liars, self-absorbed, not to be trusted and just no good. I hate to say a person is no good, but there are some people who are just bad and don't care about others, and I had become involved with one. I listened to what he had to say and told him I would let him know the next day. I had a lot to think about. I hate to say that I hated him, but I know I dislike everything about him, and he was the worst mistake I made in my life. We all make mistakes but some are worse than others. I know for sure that nobody can say that about me. I had this man around my grandchildren and thought he would be a good role model. He had a past and had been in jail before, but I thought he had turned his life around. I was wrong.

Wait until you read the next chapters in this sad story.

2ND CHAPTER

The first chapter was bad, and the second gets worse. I should have left the minute he started going out with this woman; our relationship was over. I couldn't see that at the time. So, I was trying to save the relationship by doing everything I knew he liked, which was wrong because I was still in love with him. So, I left the shelter and had them to bring the POD back with the all the furniture that belonged to me. I was raised in a religious family and had a family member that was an evangelist, and I was taught to do the right thing at all time. As I said the Lord was calling me and God was working on changing all of my desired but, I was still being led by the devil, thinking that I could trust him again to be a stand-up guy. That was crazy because he was being led by devil too, and he did not grow up like I did with the Lord in my family praying for me.

I was being called by the Lord, but I still could not see it. If you never buy anything new or upgrade your car or furniture people would start to wonder what you are doing with your money. We both had jobs at one time and should have something to show for it. I would buy things with my money because I didn't believe in spending all money on drugs, and we would have argument about me spending money on furniture, clothes, computers, and food. The Lord will bring you to the end of yourself, so you will know that you need a Savior in your life and that is what he was doing. When I went to the shelter and it was supposed to be the start of my new life but without the Lord in my life, it wasn't going to work. I still had to find that out. I had found a job and had started to look for an apartment. I couldn't live in the shelter. It was a bad place to live, and I never lived like that before. It was hard to adjust to this. Carl was calling me all day and night begging me to come back, and l miss my pet too much. So, I let the devil trick me again and went back to that house. I didn't have to worry about her, because she had problems of her own with her husband now that he was aware of what had been going on. After I returned from living in the shelter, my pet became ill and died within two weeks. That was also a sign, and I still couldn't see it that the relationship was over. We were still on drugs, and he was still the same person who wasn't to be trusted at all. I started watching different ministries and listening to the sermon. I knew there was a better life waiting for me. As I said, I was raised in the word and knew that I was living in sin and when I would talk to him about it. He would say things like he wouldn't marry me and would act like I wasn't good enough for him after he made certain promises to me if I would come back (HA!) another lie. He would say that he wouldn't go to hell because we won't marry. I always knew he was a heathen, but I thought he would come around by the time we hit our sixties. I was heartbroken over the death of my pet that I started looking for another puppy, and he said he would buy another one for me. That is why I believe he loved me, but he was a hypocrite and not to be believed. Now, the job that I had wanted hired me on for full-time, but I couldn't take it because of the drug test. There were many jobs I had to let go because of that. He would not stop using so I could get the job. That would have help me. I did that for him when he needed my help so he could get a job. So, I had to quit and look for another job, so we went and picked up another puppy. I thought that would make me happy and fill the hole in my heart. I didn't have to worry about her anymore since her husband was watching her every move. She would call every now and then to threaten me, but I would just hang up.

The next chapter is about the move from the street where all those events happened and his retirement that was going to make our life better. This was the beginning of how treacherous he would become. Just when you think it couldn't any worse it does.

3ʳᴅ CHAPTER
MY DELIVERANCE

After everything he had put me through, you would think he would be a better person to me. I wasn't so lucky. He received his pension money from a job he had before I met him, which was enough to buy a house without having a mortgage payment, and he would start to receive social security payments. I should have realized then this wasn't going anywhere because he didn't put my name on the mortgage of the house. He said that I could stay there as long as I wanted. That was his way of getting around not putting my name on the mortgage after we have been together for twenty-three years. There was no future for me in that arrangement, nothing in writing. If anything should happen to him, his family would get the house and put me out. I didn't realize that this new situation wasn't good for me until later on; I wasn't in a good frame of mind. Things started looking up for us; I had a job and was making some good money too. I mean really good money. I would bring home at least six hundred dollars or more every weekend, and it all went to drugs. Then, it started: the beginning of the end. The house he had chosen wasn't in a good location, and the neighbor was horrible and a drug dealer. The Lord had me trade in the car I had that was costing a lot of money, and I quit the job that I had bringing in all that money. Of course, he was upset. It was a job I did not want and it would not get me anywhere no future and I was not willing to spend all the money in drugs. God is so amazing and how the devil will use different events against you and how God will protect you. He was wiping the things I used to do away from me. I did not want them anymore or that lifestyle. I was so desperate to leave that house that one of my old co-worker, who knew what I was going through, offered to give me a loan. I could pay her back later and could get out of that house that was not in God's plan for me. Well, it turned out she couldn't be trusted either. I was doing this on my own efforts and not the plans God had for me. So, I started looking for another job while going on unemployment. I didn't have the money that I had before, so he really started to show his true colors again. I would spend a lot of the money on our habit when I was working and couldn't smoke the drugs because I would have to go to work so he was able to smoke most of it. When I got off of work, I would have to buy more. When he worked at night, I wasn't allowed to smoke any of it till he came home. If I did, there would be a fight. I started watching the T.V. ministries. The abuse was getting to be too much and now I didn't have money to help buy drugs. There was no sex life after the affair. I really didn't want him touching me, and I didn't trust him anymore. The Lord was calling me more and more and the more I watch the TV ministries, I knew I needed to answer the Lord. I wanted to go to heaven and nothing down here was worth me going to hell for. He didn't want to go to church and wasn't going to marry me. I started paying tithes and reading the bible. I knew I had to get another job and take a drugs test, so I stopped getting high, which was easy. The Lord took the taste of drugs out of my mouth.

Carl had treated me so bad when I would smoke with him, he would steal the drugs from me even if I bought it. He would accuse me of smoking the joint the wrong way and make the joint burn the wrong way. We had a fight one day about a little bit of the drugs that was left that I had purchased, so he blew it into my face. He started telling me that he wanted me out of his house that day. So, I started packing, and my daughter-in-law came over and helped me. He didn't stop calling me names because she was there; he said some horrible things. It was easy for me to quit after that day. I didn't have a job or anywhere to go. I wasn't going back to the shelter. My daughter-in-law didn't want her kids to come over any more and neither did I after that day. I know now that the devil was using him to come against me, which helped me to know that I needed the Lord in my life. It was time for me to give my life to the Lord. It was never the same again. My deliverance was all I could pray for everyday along with peace as long as I had to stay there. I had to start all over again. This was the beginning. I listened to all the ministries, read the bible every day, and tried to stay away from him as much as possible. If he asked for a ride or to cook something and I didn't do it, he would tell me to get out and call me all kinds of names. He had already run away all of my friends and most of my family. Holidays and birthdays were a nightmare. He wouldn't even acknowledge Mother's day or my birthday. He wouldn't even say Merry Christmas or Happy New Year. I had to endure these holidays for a couple more years. In the bible, it said about being unequal yoke. I always thought it was about one person being saved and the other not being saved. That is not what the means. You can be two people coming from two different worlds. I would have never treated him or anyone else the way he was treating me- the mean and nasty things he would do to me again. He stopped hitting because he didn't want to go to jail, so he use mental abuse by not talking to me and not doing anything that he knew I would like and he stop be around for most of the time. I found a part-time job with a program working four hours a day, five days a week. I had to start somewhere so I could get an apartment and get out of his house. Each time we had a fight, it would be worse than the one before. I felt this was a start that the Lord was working until I could get a full- time job. Carl showed me no respect and would scream and yell in and outside the house and in the car. One day when I came back from work, he was at the house. I had not seen him since he went to work the night before and never came back after work. He wanted me to drive him to get drugs, and I said no that he should have the people he was with the night before to take him to get his drugs. Remember, I had stop smoking a while ago. That was a big mistake, because that only made him mad and he spit in my face and called me all kinds of names outside. I never had any one spit on me before and as you can guess, this hurt so much that this was a person I thought I would be with until we die. I thought he loved me at one time and would never do anything to hurt me. I knew after that event that I had to leave and as soon as possible. I called for prayers and continue to ask the Lord for help and deliverance from the living situation. The Lord answer my prayers and gave me a full- time job. The pay wasn't that great, but it was a start since Carl ask me about paying him rent. This wasn't going to happen. He would use the money to buy drugs, and I wasn't going to let that happen. The Lord gave me that job so I could get out of the house, not help him buy drugs. I told him I would continue to pay the cable bill and that was all. I needed to be able to watch and hear the ministries. I passed the entire drug tests and the criminal background check. One good thing about the job: there was a lot of overtime, but it would still take a long time to get the money I needed for an apartment-- first month and last month rent. At the job I would have to wait a year for a raise. So, I was looking at another year in this house and the abuse when even he felt like it. He started leaving the house every Saturday night and not returning until the next day maybe not even then. He would tell a lie about helping his family with their business. I always thought this was in his planning to get me to leave, another way to make life horrible by ignoring me. I would spend all of my time alone with the dog. Remember, he works at night during the week and now he would leave every Saturday night. No one to talk to and nothing to do but, go to work and take care of the dog. I never thought he could be this cruel than he was before. This helps me get over wanting a relationship with him because he was never around, and I was able to get closer to the Lord and read and study the bible. The Lord started to comfort my heart and guide me in the way I should go. One day, I went to work, and my Manager was holding meeting with employees about us receiving a raise for the work we were performing at that time, and it was a good raise. You know this was God working on my behalf and making a way for me to get out of there. In the past, I would rush to the house and tell Carl about this news. I would never call the house a home because it was never my home. The raise was to start in the next pay date, but it didn't happen, and I was very disappointed. I wanted to start saving as soon as possible. So, every pay day the same thing happened no raised in my pay and my Manager was working on getting the money for me, but it did not happen for six months. This was God's plan, and I didn't understand until now. I had several of God's tools with me: the Christian program, the word, the teaching that I was able hear on a daily basis, calling for prayer when needed, and the DVD of Christian songs (I have been Changed is of the one songs). Years ago, I was in contact with a young Christian woman who sent me her DVD of wonderful songs and at the time, I wasn't even into Christian music thing about being saved. I kept it, and I can't tell you what it has done for me. There were so many songs to comfort me. When I traded in my old car and purchased a new one, it came with Sirius radio station that played Christian songs, which was a blessing. That became the only station I listened to. They played songs like Power in the Name of Jesus. At the time, my daughter-in-law was in a program to buy a house and suggested that I go to the program to see if I would be able to qualify. So, I went and did qualify, but you had to go to classes and needed to have a down payment or some savings. I didn't have either one. I started working on the classes and praying for the money to come through from my job. I felt like this was going to take a long time, and I was in a hurry. I was so desperate that I went to another company hoping they could help me faster. That is when I found out that the government helps with down payment, and you have to have good credit. I had my work cut out for me. That was another thing that I had let go by being with him. I didn't take care of my credit history. I had to start cleaning up my credit before I could move out and save some money. I still had to pick him up from work and take him to buy drugs every night. Carl would not put gas in the car and if I would say something about it, he would tell me off and tell me to leave his house because I didn't pay anything. One night after picking him up from work, I was parking the car and a car was behind me. He got out the car and went to the car that was behind me. He started arguing with the person in the car, so I got out the car to see what was going on. It was a woman telling him off. She was saying that it wasn't her calling me on my phone. I had told him that someone was calling me, and he must have given them my number. She was upset because she said it wasn't her calling me, and that there were other women who had my number. Some of them would start describing the house and the bathroom and would talk about how they liked my pet when they called me on my cell phone. There was only one way they knew these things. They had to be in the house while I was at work. I was in a fight with the devil and every time he had a chance, he would come against me by using him. I told you he would leave every Saturday night and if he would fall asleep, that is when my phone would ring. The calls would be from women telling me to send him out the house and when he didn't come out, they would come up and ring the doorbell. I had to live through this every weekend along with the isolation. I use thing time to get closer to the Lord and read the word. I continue to listen to the services on the TV and praying for my deliverance. Living in fornication for twenty- three years meant I could not take communion on Sundays, and that was another reason I had to get out of there. It was a new year coming, and I was sure the Lord was working it out for me. I couldn't continue to live like this; it was too hard. I was still expecting the money from my job and on one of my pay checks, it was there and in lump sum. The Lord provides this for me right on time. If I had received this money a couple months around Christmas, I would have spent some of it on gifts. Things were falling into God's plan, and Carl couldn't see it. There was a CD I played all the time when he was in the car (Things Won't Stay this way) and if he would listen to the words, he would have seen it coming. He would have realized that you can't treat God's people the way he did. You can't go around stepping on people the way he was doing to me. Almost every month he would tell me to get out his house, but he didn't know what was going on and how the Holy Ghost was guiding my every step. This is the best part of my stories and how the Lord was working it out for me and had a place already for me. As the months went on, I was still taking the classes and learning how I can become a home owner. I felt like I was in a dream from the beginning until now writing the end to this story. It is still hard to believe what happened and how it happened the next couple months. Carl never stop abusing me every chance he got. The devil continues to use him against me. On one of our trips to his drug dealer he informed me that I was an ungrateful B for everything he had done for me. I asked him what had he done for me; his answer was letting me live in his house for free and the lump sum of money he gave me when he got is pension money. I couldn't believe the amount he said he gave me., I wanted him to show me the proof, but he couldn't because now gave me a dime. If he had given me what he said, I would have taken the money and moved out then. I felt like I was in a movie, because the Lord took over my life and guided my path. This was in the beginning of May and one of the requirements for attending the program for homeowners was to get a realtor to show me houses. The first one I contacted didn't work out, and I was very upset. The Lord was with me, and I can remember praying every morning and calling the hotline for prayer: Matt. 18:19. I would say every minute that I believe and I am the righteous of God. Every day was a nightmare. I would see things when I came back to house after work that he had people in the house while I was at work using the bathroom taking a shower. Sometime on the weekends, he would come home in a car filled with women. When he would leave again on Saturday night, I would get a call the next morning from a woman telling me what they did the night before. I was being tortured every weekend, so the Lord had me call another real estate agent who turned out to be the right one. I had never done this before, and I didn't know how things would go. She started showing different houses and the third one she showed me, I knew it was the one. Things were happening fast. She made an offer and in two days, it was accepted. The closing was set for the next month which was in July. Remember, the Lord had already provided the money I would need months before. The only thing I was worried about was moving day. If he would know, there would be trouble. He would tell me to move almost every day, but the devil was working in him and would use him to come against me if he was there when I would be moving. He treated me like I was an outcast in his world. All the things that had happened to us and we lived through didn't matter to him. I would have never thought he would treat me this way. I would have never treated him this way. There were a lot of things that happened that he caused, and I never held it against him all of those years. He would go to jail at least once a week in the beginning of our relationship and I would stand by him and get him out. When you love someone, you go through the good and bad with them. That is what you do, and it is the right thing to do. I thank God for loving me and for being with me through all of this. I had heard about people treating other people like this, but I never thought he would be one of them, and people in my family could not believe it either. It was getting closer to my moving day, and I was preparing for it by making the arrangements without him knowing. Looking back on this still hurts my heart to know that all those years were for nothing. I had to go through that to get to this point. I thank God He brought me through it because if I had not found my way to Him, what would have become of me? Look at how many people have not found the Lord and killed themselves or are living on the streets in this world, and that could have been me. I thank Him every day for helping and giving me the desire of his heart for me. I signed my mortgage paper and received my keys, next was the moving day. When I first started writing this short story some four years ago, I didn't realize the love of God, what he would do for me, and how he would guide my life. If I only believed in His mercy and love for me, that Jesus gave his life for me before I was born, and how the Holy Ghost would walk and talk to me daily.

It is a year later and there was more that God had to show me. It was like I was watching a movie of my life. First, God provided a job for me then, He gave me a promotion at the same time. The job was supposed to go to someone else who had been at the company before me. They left town for another job, and the manager, who gave me the job, resigned two weeks after she promoted me. The last step was to get me out of that house so I would be able to take communion on Sunday. That was the best thing and the desire of my heart. I stopped having any physical relationship with him after he started running around with women, calling me so many names, and finally after he spit in my face because I wouldn't take him to buy drugs. It was moving week, and I was very nervous about it. I had scheduled it for that Friday, and it was Monday. I was at that house waiting for him to come home from work, and it was getting late into the night. My phone rang and the person on the phone let me know he wouldn't be coming home that night, it was the police. The Lord had created a situation that would keep him out of the house for a couple of days. He was in jail. I thought about moving the next day, but I had made all the arrangement for the end of the week. This was the best part of the story and how God works. He didn't come back until that Wednesday, and he thought he had lost his job but I had called his boss to make sure he would keep it. Remember, he works at night and also, the police took his phone too. The phone was especially important because he was friends with the people next door, and I was afraid that they would call him and tell him that I was moving on Friday. The Lord will take care of all your needs. So, I was able to move in peace and was gone before he came home. The Lord gave me the desire of His heart, and it is a beautiful house: everything I ever wanted and no one is telling me to get out. I also took the dog, and he is enjoying it too. I couldn't leave him there not knowing what would happen to him. I thank the Lord every day for loving me and supplying all my needs. Looking back on everything that I went through and the dreams that I had for my life, I know that without the love of the Lord I would have never made it. I had so much trust in Carl and believed he was a good person. Because of the Lord in my life, I can forgive him and go on with my life. Some days it is hard, because I relive those days. That is when I read the word or listen to a sermon. I know the Lord has nothing but the best for me because he saved my life and loves me. Because of my salvation and my daily walk in God, Jesus Christ, and the Holy Ghost who saved my life and me and the dog is doing fined and living a peaceful live.

Only believe in the Lord!

www.ingramcontent.com/pod-product-compliance
Lightning Source LLC
LaVergne TN
LVHW021739060526
838200LV00052B/3372